Sisters

Sisters

A play by Wendy Lill

Talonbooks • Vancouver • 1991

Published with the assistance of the Canada Council

Talonbooks
201 - 1019 East Cordova Street
Vancouver, British Columbia
Canada V6A 1M8

Designed by Sally Bryer Mennell. This book was set in 10/12 Palacio by Pièce de Résistance Ltée., and printed and bound in Canada by Hignell Printing Ltd.

Second Printing: April 1995

Canadian Cataloguing in Publication Data
Lill, Wendy, 1950-
  Sisters

  A play.
  ISBN 0-88922-289-4

  I. Title.
PS8573.I42S5   1991   C812'.54   C91-091441-9
PR9199.3.L54S5 1991

In memory of
Edwin Henry Lill

Sisters was first performed at the Ship's Company Theatre in Parrsboro, Nova Scotia, in August 1989 with the following cast:

Young Mary	Krista Wells
Sister Gabriel	Mary-Colin Chisholm
Mother Agnes	Gay Hauser
Sister Mary	Nicola Lipman
Louis	John Beale
Stein	Michael Keating

Directed by Mary Vingoe.
Original score by Paul Cram.
Set design by Stephen Osler.
Costume design by Krista Levy.

CHARACTERS

Y. MARY (YOUNG MARY)

LOUIS, *confident, horny*

GABRIEL

AGNES

MARY

STEIN

ACT ONE *takes place in 1969 in a county lock-up in rural Nova Scotia; in 1950 at a nearby farm; and during the late 1950s, and late '60s in an Indian residential school, also nearby.*

ACT TWO *takes place for the most part in 1969 in the county lock-up and in the residential school in the late '60s, with flashbacks to farm, last 1950.*

SISTERS *is a reconstruction/memory play. Mary's mind and emotions are the mechanisms which hold these realities/memories apart. At times of intensity, they begin to merge.*

There are three separate realities which all radiate from the central character MARY in her efforts to reconstruct past events and lost dreams which led to her act of burning down the school. MARY is seen in the present (1969) with STEIN, but also as YOUNG MARY, a 17-year-old farm girl with a young man named LOUIS, and then later, as a young nun, interacting with Sisters GABRIEL and AGNES.

As the world of the play is the world of Mary's mind, fixed realistic sets depicting the different ''realities'' are not recommended; they are better treated in a fluid fashion.

Heightened sound is very important in this play.

Act One

SISTER MARY is standing in silhouette watching a fire which is destroying an Indian residential school. The sound of the fire is horrible and frightening but along with it we hear native children singing hymns. One voice begins to rise more clearly and purely than the others, then it is overtaken by a strain of jazz. The year is 1969.

Black

Light grows on Y. MARY, 17, hanging laundry meticulously and singing her favorite popular jazz song. LOUIS is trying to interest her in him instead.

Light grows on MOTHER AGNES and SISTER GABRIEL at the Indian Residential School, several months before the burning.

Light grows on MARY in a bare room, with table and chair. Dressed in a simple grey skirt and shirt, she is standing with her back to the audience, looking out of a window.

GABRIEL: *Standing*
> I keep thinking about the floors. We had the shiniest floors in North America

AGNES:
> Don't think about it.

MARY:
> Think about it.

GABRIEL:
> We're like a wave moving where God blows us aren't we, Mother Agnes . . . the school and then . . . do you think the tulips will come up without us watching them?

9

LOUIS moves closer to Y. MARY.

Y. MARY: *(breaks off singing)*
There's another verse but I can never get the words Can you?

LOUIS:
I never try. I turn the radio off whenever that song comes on.

Y. MARY:
How come?

LOUIS:
'Cause I'm sick of hearing women SING about it. I get this ache, Mary, and then I get this panicky feeling that I'm gonna be left high and dry.

MARY:
We do a little bit, Louis.

LOUIS:
We don't DO IT at all! You're too busy talking or singing or hanging the perfect laundry. *(LOUIS pulls the pins out of her hair)* And there's only one week left to . . . .

Y. MARY turns to him and they start necking.
Sound of a train, fading into sound of children playing.
Sounds grow loud, distorted.

AGNES:
And who have we here today?

MARY:
One of the Simons from Cape Breton. This one's Betty.

AGNES:
Papers all in order?

MARY:
Yes, Mother Agnes.

GABRIEL:

    Did she like watching the big bright engine up front
    when it went round the bends?

MARY:

    Apparently she sat quite still.

AGNES:

    Does she speak any English?

MARY:

    Mr. Cameron heard some swear words.

GABRIEL:

    She looks serene.

MARY: *(sharply)*

    Don't believe it. She kicked him all the way up the lane.

    Y. MARY pulls away for air.

Y. MARY:

    That's far enough. I've got to go take care of the twins.

LOUIS:

    Take care of me.

Y. MARY:

    I've got to clean the house before Father Mackie arrives.

LOUIS:

    Just once. Something to remember.

Y. MARY:

    Stop it, Louis.

LOUIS:

    No one'll know.

Y. MARY:

    I'll know. God will know.

11

LOUIS:

> God won't mind. It's just horny old priests like Father Mackie that mind.

Y. MARY:

> Louis!

LOUIS making another move on her.

Y. MARY: *(struggling with him)*
> Why are you doing this?

LOUIS:

> 'Cause I'm trying to change your mind girl. 'Cause once we do it, you'll wanna get married and have children and . . .

Y. MARY: *(finally breaks away)*
> I'm gonna be a nun, Louis. I'm not changing my mind!

LOUIS: Frustrated
> Jesus Christ!

Y. MARY:

> I'm gonna be beautiful and serene and peaceful like Sister Margaret in Primary with the tiny hands.

LOUIS:

> You got great big hands Mary.

Y. MARY:

> I'm gonna teach the poor Indians over at the government school.

LOUIS:

> Who'd rather make baskets and hunt rabbits. Why can't people just be the way they bloody well want?

Y. MARY:

> 'Cause you don't always know what's best for you.

LOUIS:

    And who's supposed to tell ya?

Y. MARY:

    You're supposed to accept certain things on faith and
    the beauty of God's plan will some day come clear
    to you.

LOUIS:

    That's goobledegook.

    LOUIS starts kissing her neck.

LOUIS:

    I've got this ache again, girl. Don't you?

    Y. MARY pulls away, gets up.

MARY: *(remembering, whispers)*
    Yes.

    STEIN has entered the room where MARY is standing.
    STEIN looks at her for a long time, finally clears his throat,
    marches in briskly.

STEIN:

    Hello, my name's Joel Stein. I'm the duty counsel
    here in town. I've been asked to come and see you
    since I gather you don't want the Sisters' law firm
    involved. Is that correct?

    MARY tenses but doesn't turn. STEIN opens briefcase,
    takes out papers, then looks up at her.

STEIN:

    I'm not sure what to call you. Ms. Mary Buchanan,
    Sister Buchanan, ah, Mary of Jesus, Miss Nun Mary? I
    don't mean to be ignorant. I'm just sort of . . . Jewish.

    MARY doesn't answer.

STEIN:

I guess Sister Mary will have to do.

There have been several calls from a Mother Agnes Parker. She wants to know how you're doing. She's convinced that there's been a misunderstanding, that you really do want their lawyer representing you. Do you have any messages for Mother Agnes? Has there been a misunderstanding?

MARY shakes her head vehemently.

STEIN:

How ARE you doing?

MARY looks at him, then back down, turning a metal cup in her hand.

Y. MARY is standing looking up at a large cross. SISTER GABRIEL and AGNES are watching her.

GABRIEL:

Who is she, Aggie?

AGNES:

A simple devout girl from the next county.

GABRIEL:

With the voice of an angel.

AGNES:

And the gait of a workhorse.

GABRIEL:

I love her youth.

AGNES:

I love her grandmother's butter knives. All nine of them.

GABRIEL:

That's probably all the dowry they could afford. Don't be such a—forgive me Father—unholy bitch.

AGNES:
> And don't you fill her head with things. Leave well
> enough alone.
>
> *AGNES approaches Y. MARY. GABRIEL carries a
> novitiate habit.*

AGNES:
> And now that you are about to become one of us, I'll
> help you look the part. We can talk this time but this
> is the last time. Do you understand?
>
> *GABRIEL begins to help Y. MARY dress*

Y. MARY:
> I think so, Sister Agnes.

GABRIEL:
> Alone.
>
> *STEIN notices that MARY has bent the metal cup out of
> shape.*

STEIN:
> I'll take that to mean no messages.

AGNES:
> As your novitiate mistress, my job is to submerge your
> personality, as much as we know of it at this early
> age. You've been at the Motherhouse for three years.
> How did you find that?

Y. MARY:
> It was heavenly! We all had our own rooms and even
> our own closets. I made a new friend from Omaha,
> Nebraska and another from Mexico named Margaretia
> Felicia who was teaching me Spanish . . .
>
> *GABRIEL is enjoying her account.*

AGNES: *(pulling Mary's hair back, cuts her off)*
> This process will be helped along without all of this.

line coming up

LOUIS: *(only OLDER MARY hears)*
    You've got beautiful hair.

Y. MARY: *(subdued)*
    I'll be glad to be rid of it.

AGNES:
    It will be shaved once a month . . . You'll be thankful
    when summer comes round and you're simmering
    under all of these layers. Do you come from a large
    family?

Y. MARY:
    Eight brothers and six sisters.

AGNES:
    And your mother? Is she still with us?

Y. MARY:
    She died when the twins were born.

GABRIEL/AGNES:
    God bless her and keep her.

AGNES:
    Did you leap or were you pushed?

Y. MARY:
    I don't understand?

AGNES:
    Did you choose to come or did you get roped into it?

Y. MARY:
    I chose, Sister Agnes. Even when I was young, I took
    baskets to the needy with my mother. I've always
    wanted to help others.

AGNES:
    And when did it happen?

Y. MARY:
        What?

AGNES:
        When did you get the Divine Call?

GABRIEL:
        When I was twelve, I started dreaming about living
        inside the head of a flower. And all above me there
        was blue sky and white birds soaring then changing
        into clouds.

        Y. MARY staring at GABRIEL

AGNES:
        Let's let little Mary talk, shall we?

Y. MARY: *(uneasy)*
        That's all I have to say.

AGNES:
        I see.   *(studies her)*   Are there any regrets?

        Y. MARY shakes her head.

AGNES:
        Speak up.

Y. MARY:
        No.

AGNES:
        Nothing you'll miss?

Y.MARY:
        No.

AGNES:
        When I was about your age, I had a good job in an
        office with three people under me. Then one day, in
        the middle of a conversation with an employee, I
        looked around and all I saw was empty space. And all

I felt was an immense loneliness. Soon after, I heard the Call and I had to take it. I cursed a lot, I broke off an engagement, my parents disowned me. That was 20 years ago. But I still yearn for my adding machine. And an Export A cigarette.

Y. MARY:
Really?

AGNES:
We're like icebergs Mary, so much is hidden, so many wants we don't even know are there, lying in wait to smash things up. But you've got to focus on one thing alone and you've got to aim for it.

GABRIEL:
Bull's-eye.

AGNES:
There will be dark hours when you will doubt your faith, you'll just have to hold on, ride them through. You must strip your heart of personal concerns, your wants, your memories, all your silly vanities so that you can focus on your true calling. The love of God. You're sure this is what you want?

Y. MARY:
Yes.

AGNES:
There are rules for everything from washing your face to looking sideways.

GABRIEL:
Too many rules.

AGNES:
You have to learn them then forget them. They'll just become second nature; almost involuntary, like blinking your eyes.

Y. MARY:
>I don't mind rules.

AGNES:
>The rules are there so that we can avoid contamination
>from the world, so that we can focus all of our love on
>easing suffering.

GABRIEL:
>Love.

AGNES:
>You've been missioned here at St. Theresa. Father
>Martin is our principal and our confessor. The Lord is
>our master. The Government is our employer and
>someday, I'm going to be Mother Superior. Is this
>truly what you want?

Y. MARY: *(solemnly)*
>Yes.

AGNES:
>Do you take this life, Mary Buchanan?

Y. MARY:
>I do.

AGNES:
>Good. And now I will endeavour to make you sweetly
>dead to the world.

>*STEIN looks up from his file.*

STEIN:
>It says here you were found by an RCMP officer in the
>field directly beside the school "apparently fixated by
>the sight of the flames."

>*AGNES starts leading Y. MARY away. GABRIEL stands
>watching.*

19

GABRIEL:
> Vaya con Dios

STEIN:
> When Constable Allen attempted to draw you away
> to safety, you said "It's all right. The worst is over."
> And then lifting your hands up to his face in "sort of
> a cupped motion" you suggested that he smell the
> fragrance of your hands. Is that correct? Not
> understanding the meaning of the remark, Constable
> Allen did same at which point you uttered
> "Gasoline, officer. I take full responsibility." Does
> this sound . . . familiar?

> *MARY doesn't answer.*

STEIN:
> If you don't remember saying this stuff, I'd say that
> Constable Allen's been sampling the drugs he's been
> confiscating.

> *MARY looks up at him.*

STEIN:
> Just kidding. Constable Allen is very straight. I guess
> you brought the gasoline with you. Maybe from the
> gas station down the highway. Did you bring the
> gasoline? (*looking at his notes*)
> You taught at St. Theresa's School, didn't you? For
> almost fifteen years . . . right up until they shut it
> down, slammed up the FOR SALE sign.
> (*almost to himself*) One mean old grey stone school.
> Millions of windows, children not included. (*to MARY*)
> And now you're in Truro, I see, teaching
> geography and history to grade seven students
> at a junior . . .

> *MARY slams her hand down on the table.*

MARY:
> Silence! I want silence.

STEIN: *(after stunned silence)*
> You sound like a teacher.

MARY:
> That is what I am.

STEIN:
> Well I'm a lawyer. I can't give you silence. It's against
> my nature. And it goes over like a lead balloon in
> court. So let's talk, Sister. Where do you want to
> start? Fifteen years. That's a long time to do anything.
> What was it like in there? Kids these days are holy
> terrors. They say teachers are under a lot of pressure.
> Was it ah . . . you know . . . pressure that made
> you . . . .

AGNES: *(begins under STEIN)*
> Hail Mary, full of Grace, the Lord is with thee, blessed
> art thou amongst women and blessed is the fruit of
> thy womb Jesus.

STEIN:
> Sister Mary, I can't help you if you won't talk to me.

GABRIEL/Y.MARY: *(in unison)*
> Holy Mary Mother of God, pray for us sinners now
> and at the hour of our death.

> *Lights up on Y.MARY in prayer stall looking heavenward.*

Y.MARY: *(continuing)* . . .
> Forgive me Lord for I was lighthearted. When I asked
> Peter Solace why he had his head stuck out the
> window he told me he was listening to the sap
> running up the tree—and I laughed at that.

GABRIEL:
> I pray that the new little Mary will hear the voices of
> the children . . . and help bring sunshine into this
> soggy dungeon.

Y.MARY:

I pray that they will be able to hold High C for a full count of five . . . and learn their multiplication tables.

AGNES:

Thank you for the new life and hope in our new sister Mary. May her manner improve and her spirit settle.

GABRIEL:

Forgive me for teasing Aggie but I can't help myself. Sometimes she just seems so . . . puffed up.

Y. MARY:

I could never learn mine.

AGNES:

Forgive me my overwhelming desire for mashed potatoes . . .

Y. MARY:

But above all I pray that you'll be my constant companion as I strive to love these poor souls.

GABRIEL:

And that Father Martin will order more poetry for the library.

AGNES:

But until I conquer my desire, may I be the last one served at night and may the good Sisters leave me the lion's share.

Y. MARY:

But above all I pray that you'll be my constant companion and that the warmth of your love will light my way as I head down the road to perfection.

STEIN is watching MARY sitting, her head bobbing up and down, obviously praying.

GABRIEL:
God bless the children.

AGNES:
God bless my reverend Sisters . . . and our mission.

Y. MARY:
God bless Mommy and may we meet up again some day in heaven, in Jesus' name . . .

STEIN loosens his tie.

STEIN:
Whew! It's hot in here. Mind if I take off my jacket?

MARY:
I prefer that you didn't.

STEIN:
I appreciate your honesty. *(a pause)* Why don't you tell me about the fire? *(no response)* Fires! I like fires. In fact, I'm nuts about them. Love the sound, the smell of them. Fires are exciting. They're conclusive. I like to think about them starting up real small with tiny bits of paper or a spark in a rag, then climbing up stairs and into beds and closets and bookcases. When I was a kid, I used to picture my father's house burning down, then gone, nothing left. Nothing. And everyone crowded around me, sympathizing, giving me things . . . baseball cards, marbles, comic books. Even my enemies at school. At least once a week I'd get into my burn-down-dad's-house trip. Should probably see a shrink about it some day but who's got the time?

STEIN notices that MARY is staring at him.

STEIN:
Sister Mary? Is that a spark of . . . .

MARY looks down quickly.

23

AGNES: *(only MARY hears)*
> Curiosity is to be avoided at all costs.

STEIN:
> I guess not.

> *Y. MARY is moving her finger up and down the window pane, looking out of the window, thinking of the past. Lonely. The silence is palpable. GABRIEL enters.*

GABRIEL:
> Tracing raindrops. I used to do that too when I was a little girl, when my mind was wandering far away. It's all right to talk, Sister Mary. The raindrops can't hear you. Don't you want to know anything about me?

Y.MARY:
> Sister Agnes says that the rule of silence is to be observed so that we can better hear God.

GABRIEL:
> Sometimes Agnes is full of old rope!

> *Y. MARY laughs. GABRIEL joins her at the window.*

GABRIEL:
> I wonder if the stone wall is washed away again? I guess we'll find out soon enough. The cows will start wandering in. I remember once looking up in pottery class and there was a big brown and white spotted face looking in the window. The silly old things always seem to run the wrong way.

> *Y. MARY laughs.*

GABRIEL:
> You're from a farm, aren't you? With rolling hills, and barns and bright yellow haystacks?
> "Season of mists and mellow fruitfulness, close bosom-friend of the maturing sun" – Keats.

I grew up in Boston. I never even SAW a cow until I
came here!

Y.MARY:

    I don't believe that!

GABRIEL:

    It's true!

Y. MARY:

    No!

GABRIEL:

    Cross my heart and hope to die! Step in a crack,
break my mother's back. Forgive me Sister. I've been
listening to the children in the yard.

Y. MARY:

    I was just thinking about my mother. She loved rainy
days because it meant no laundry. Then we didn't
feel guilty about sitting by the radio listening to the
station from New York. I knew every song. I'd even
stand in front of the mirror and pretend I was the
one singing.

GABRIEL: *(starts singing)*

    "I'm singing in the rain, just singing in the rain,
What a glorious feeling, I'm happy again."

Y. MARY:

    It's against the rules to sing that kind of song, isn't it?

GABRIEL:

    Oh, I don't follow that rule either. Sister Agnes follows
the rules. I break them. How do you like it here?

Y. MARY: *(hesitates)*

    It's the life I've chosen.

GABRIEL:

    Oh, say something truthful! You're young. It's still
permitted.

Y. MARY:

>I find the silence . . . horrible. The words keep building up inside 'til I can barely think for the noise.

GABRIEL:

>But at least you're teaching music. You've got a chance to open up your lungs and sing!

Y. MARY:

>Thank heavens.

GABRIEL:

>How do you find them? The little Indians. Are they what you expected?

Y. MARY:

>I'm not sure.

GABRIEL:

>They love lunch, don't they?

Y. MARY: *(laughs)*

>Yes!

GABRIEL:

>When they start eating, they don't know how to stop.

Y. MARY:

>When they stop working, it's impossible to start them up again.

GABRIEL:

>I never know when I'm going to have to wait a century for a simple answer. But they're good children, Mary. I think that the sound that God loves the most is the sound of their singing. Sometimes, when I listen to it long enough, I think it IS the sound of God.

Y. MARY:

>Please Sister Gabriel!

GABRIEL:

>It's true! And I think that the sound that he hates the most, is the dogs barking. Because that means one of them has run away.

Y. MARY:

>But they have to be brought back.

GAB:

>Do they?

Y. MARY:

>That's our mission. To civilize them.

GABRIEL:

>I'll tell you a secret. I have my own little mission. I do little things to make them happy, to benefit them . . . just in little ways. They're only children after all. God's little lambs.

>*STEIN is watching MARY.*

STEIN:

>Yup . . . holy terrors. Want to talk about the kids?

Y. MARY:

>We'd better bring in the rest of the laundry.

STEIN:

>Is there ANYTHING you want to talk about?

>*MARY makes no response.*

>I guess this isn't easy for you. You're not exactly your run-of-the-mill arsonist. *(tries again)*
>I drove by the site of the school on my way over here. The trees around are all brown like the middle of October. It's eerie looking, unnatural. But the leaves will come back next year. I've seen that happen once before in a fire at Yellowstone Park when my dad and I were out discovering America. If that's any comfort.

There is no response from MARY. STEIN is getting more frustrated. He refers back to his papers.

STEIN:
> From what I see here, you were talkative right after the fire, maybe almost in shock. You said that you always lived by the rules, and that you wanted to take whatever punishment the government had to mete out since it was a substantial loss of bricks and mortar. Then apparently you said that you deserved punishment. Did you really say that?

Y. MARY is down on her hands and knees, scrubbing the floor with a small brush. AGNES is watching.

AGNES:
> Father Martin is still not pleased with the noise in the hall during prayers.

Y. MARY:
> I have tried everything to keep them quiet but they are only children.

AGNES:
> And this is first and foremost a religious community. There must be silence. Pray for grace.

Y. MARY:
> I pray for Grace.

STEIN:
> I wouldn't worry about the bricks and mortar. I'd wager the government's relieved to have it removed from the horizon.

AGNES:
> Father Martin has heard them speaking Indian. You know the rule about that.

Y. MARY:
> They mutter it. I can't stop them.

28

AGNES:

> You could wash their mouths out with soap. They'll never amount to anything speaking their native tongue.

STEIN:

> Erased from memory.

AGNES:

> Don't grimace. Ask for forgiveness for having hostile thoughts.

STEIN:

> Institutions like that have gone right out of fashion. They're an embarrassment. In fact, it reminded me of an old penitentiary on the highway to . . .

MARY:

> It was not a penitentiary! It was a . . .

AGNES:

> Don't try to defend yourself Mary.

STEIN:

> Keep talking.

AGNES:

> Don't talk back. You must learn the meaning of your vows. It's through obedience that you come to know the possibilities within you . . . what you can endure.

> *MARY shakes her head, walks away from STEIN.*

STEIN:

> Shut down again.

> *GABRIEL gives Y. MARY a piece of pottery.*

GABRIEL:

> I've made you something.

Y. MARY:

You shouldn't have. You know the rule about gifts.

GABRIEL:

I don't follow that one either. I let my children make special things for one another once a month. A treat. Once a month, they make wonderful clay fish and eagles and flowers instead of that dreadful industrial strength kitchen-ware .

Y. MARY:

You and your little missions!

GABRIEL:

Yesterday, we planted 200 tulip bulbs that I ordered from the nursery in New Brunswick. When they come up next spring, I'll just say that I thought they were onions.

Y. MARY:

That would be a lie, Sister Gabriel.

GABRIEL:

Just a little white one. It won't harm anyone, will it?

Y. MARY:

You can't eat tulips, Gabriel.

GABRIEL:

But they're so beautiful. I think they feed the soul, don't you?

Do you think God would mind if I slipped off and read the little ones Ivanhoe? They sit so quietly with their faces turned upwards almost as if I were their . . . You're not thinking that God would mind, are you?

Y. MARY:

There are rules!

GABRIEL:

But these are Father Martin's rules. Mr. Cameron's rules. Not God's rules.

Y. MARY:
>Please Sister, obedience is our vow.

GABRIEL:
>But it's not God who doesn't have the money to send them home for summer holidays.

Y. MARY:
>Sister Agnes says the money is going to pay for teeth and tonsils.

GABRIEL:
>Yes, yes, but surely one year they can have their teeth filled and the next year they can go home. At least once every other year.

Y. MARY:
>Mr. Cameron says that their mothers are unfit. There are abuses in the homes. Mr. Cameron says that what goes on out there makes life at the school seem like paradise.

GABRIEL:
>Mr. Cameron is a toad.

>*(Y. MARY laughs)*

GABRIEL:
>If this is paradise shouldn't we at least have monthly birthday parties? It's not God who cancelled their monthly birthday parties.

Y. MARY:
>Because they were getting too wild, too greedy for sweets. They couldn't sleep nights.

GABRIEL:
>I remember being greedy for sweets. Don't you?

Y. MARY:
>I was a bottomless pit!

GABRIEL:

> And we haven't gone to the devil, have we? At least not yet. Maybe what these children need is more sweets, if we want them to find religion. More sweets for everyone!

They both laugh. GABRIEL hugs Y. MARY.

GABRIEL:

> It's heaven to hug.

MARY rubs her arms. STEIN notices.

STEIN:

> Are you cold, Sister Mary? Would you like my jacket?

STEIN takes off his jacket and offers it to her.

MARY:

> No thank you.

STEIN:

> I'm hot. You're cold. Take it.

MARY:

> NO!

STEIN:

> Do you want me to leave?

MARY looks at him for a moment, then shakes her head.

STEIN:

> Well, I guess that's progress. Let's talk.

MARY shakes her head again.

STEIN:

> What do you want, Sister Mary?

MARY: *(after a while)*
> I haven't really "talked" in a long time. I'm out of practise. You talk.

STEIN:

>All right. I'll talk.
>
>When I got the call to come down here tonight I was getting a lecture from my girlfriend. She says we're not communicating. She says that I'm not open enough with my feelings, that I don't connect with people. I'm too uptight. I've got a wall around me that makes the one in Berlin look like a picket fence. And to top it all off, she doesn't like the way I blow my nose. I'm too flamboyant, too noisy. In my own uptight way, I enjoy it all too much . . . .

>*STEIN pulls out a large colourful handkerchief and blows his nose flamboyantly. MARY laughs, then puts her hand over her mouth.*

STEIN:

>Don't stop. It's nice to hear you laugh. Let's see, what else? She doesn't like the way I answer the . . . .

MARY:

>Why are you telling me all of this?

STEIN:

>Because you wanted me to talk. Didn't you? And I guess it's on my mind.

MARY:

>You're not from here are you?

STEIN:

>No. New York.

MARY:

>There's a war going on . . . and you're not in it.

STEIN:

>No. I'm not in it. I'm here with you.

>*MARY lowers her head again.*

STEIN:

>Talking to myself. I'm curious about this Mother
>Agnes. She really does want to see you.

MARY: *(shutting down again)*
>No.

STEIN:

>I never got along with my mother either.

>*AGNES comes up to Y. MARY*

AGNES: *(to Y. MARY)*
>Do you have a favorite, Sister Mary? Don't be
>nervous. You can tell me. Let me guess. The new
>girl, Alice Paul.

Y. MARY:

>How did you know?

AGNES:

>Because you gave her an extra rosary. I know
>everything that goes on. What do you like about
>Alice?

Y. MARY:

>She has perfect pitch. And she's cheerful and neat
>and well behaved. She reminds me of my little sister
>Binney.

AGNES:

>But she's not. Sister Cecile says she's been wetting
>her bed.

Y. MARY:

>Maybe it's because she's homesick.

AGNES:

>It's because she sneaks into the kitchen to get juice.
>You turned a blind eye to that.

Y. MARY:
I didn't think it was that serious.

AGNES:
Delusion is always serious. Don't lose sight of your goal Sister Mary. You're a hard worker. You've got a warm heart, but you're too eager to be liked. We're not here to be liked. We're here to raise the children up to God. God doesn't play favorites and neither should we or there will be chaos. For penance I'd like you to organize the sheet parade this week. There were fifteen last night. Ten on boys and five on girls. The numbers have started climbing again and it's time to set an example.

Y. MARY: *(pleadingly)*
Oh please . . . .

AGNES:
Pardon?

Y. MARY:
It is too mortifying.

AGNES:
You've seen it done, haven't you Sister? Line them up with their wet sheets over their heads outside the mess hall door. When Sister Cecile gives the signal for the others to bang their spoons, usher the fifteen into the front of the hall.

Y. MARY starts scratching her hand.

AGNES:
Once on the sheet parade, they'll move heaven and earth not to wet their beds again. It is truly a miracle how well it works and it saves a lot of work down in the laundry. What are you doing?

Y. MARY stops scratching.

AGNES: *(looks at her hand)*
>You should get Doctor Henderson to look at that.

MARY begins scratching her hand. STEIN notices.

STEIN:
>That's a bad rash you've got. It looks like nerves to me. Would you like me to ask a doctor to come in and see you? Sister Mary?

AGNES approaches Y. MARY.

AGNES:
>I've seen Gabriel trying to bend your ear in recreation.

Y. MARY:
>She likes to read poetry out loud.

AGNES:
>And I've seen the two of you whispering in line at dinner. That's against the rules.

Y. MARY:
>Gabriel is lonely!

AGNES:
>Don't try to defend yourself.

Y. MARY:
>Then don't keep chastising me! *(pause, more controlled)* I am no longer a novitiate, Sister Agnes. I know the rules.

AGNES:
>And I am no longer Sister Agnes. I am Mother Agnes now. And you are straying off course.

Y. MARY:
>Forgive me . . . Mother Agnes.

AGNES:

> Gabriel has reached the time in a nun's life when there are yearnings for things that will never be. Some of us are able to handle them better than others. But it doesn't help for her to become too attached to you; too dependent. Do you understand?

Y. MARY:

> Yes, Mother Agnes.

AGNES:

> Stop scratching! Gabriel must see how much she can endure and you must too. Saint Vincent de Paul tells us that if we are doing God's work, he will not forsake us.

> *GABRIEL begins her penance under, repeating it . . .*

GABRIEL:

> The body of Christ is crushed, let us learn to subdue our bodies. Our bodies must be conformed to the likeness of our Lord's wounded body . . . .

AGNES:

> Don't lose it, Mary. We must keep our eyes focused on the higher good and not succumb to the weaker emotions of loneliness and selfishness. For your penance you will kneel in front of the crucifix for two hours with your arms outstretched.

> *Y. MARY, her arms outstretched. (The prayers perhaps overlapping, floating together)*

Y. MARY:

> The body of Christ is crushed, let us learn to control our bodies. Our bodies must conform to the likeness of our Lord's wounded body . . .

AGNES:

> Hail Mary, full of Grace, the Lord is with thee, blessed art thou amongst women and blessed is the fruit of thy . . .

GABRIEL:

>God . . . when I go up to my cell at night, I don't want to open the door. I don't want to be alone in there. I want to hold someone's hand more than I want to breathe.To just hold a hand . . .

AGNES:

>I pray that I may provide solace to my beloved Sisters in their hours of need . . .

Y. MARY:

>I pray that God will end Gabriel's loneliness and that I too will feel less alone . . . .

AGNES:

>And that my piety will be further rewarded with a posting somewhere preferably of a more urban nature . . .

Y. MARY:

>And that I will not become discouraged or have unkind thoughts towards the children . . . they don't even smile at me since the sheet parade. Please God, give me serenity, confidence in my course . . .

GABRIEL:

>Seasons of mists and mellow fruitfulness!
>Close bosom friend of the maturing sun;
>Conspiring with him how to load and bless
>with fruit the vines that round the thatch-eaves run;
>To bend with apples the moss'd cottage-trees,
>And fill all fruit with ripeness to the core . . .

AGNES:

>And finally, that I would not feel jealous of the Sisterhood I see between Gabriel and Mary.

GABRIEL:

>To just hold a hand.

>*GABRIEL begins to cry quietly. Y. MARY hears her. She puts her hand out towards Gabriel. Gabriel takes it.*

STEIN:

What did you mean when you said you wanted to take full responsibility? That the worst was over?

MARY:

Leave me alone.

STEIN:

I don't think you mean that. I think there's something jammed up in there wanting to come out but it's stuck. If old Marie were here, she'd take one look at you and say you needed a backrub.

MARY:

Don't treat me like a spectacle, Mr Stein. I am a Reverend Sister of St. Anne and a teacher. I have instructed almost one thousand children who have been touched by my devotion, who look up to me, who . . . (*searching for words*)

STEIN:

Who what?

MARY:

You are a very intrusive young man.

STEIN:

Thank you.

MARY:

When I was your age, Mr. Stein, I already had a calling. I had closed the door on certain things and I had a clear path before me and I never wavered.

STEIN:

And here you are in the country lock-up with a Jewish pyromaniac draftdodger from New York. Stranded.

MARY:

Yes.

STEIN: *(a pause)*

>One thousand children. That's really impressive. It's amazing, isn't it, how many children can be influenced by one teacher; how much power she can have over them. Sister Mary?

AGNES is reading a missive from Father Martin to Y. MARY and GABRIEL.

AGNES:

>Mr. Cameron has finished his tour. He wasn't pleased with their manual skills. I'm afraid we are no longer to have music lessons. They are an indulgence. More practical arts, more sewing, more axe-handle making.

Y. MARY gasps.

GABRIEL:

>But I thought the point was to move them towards the finer . . .

AGNES:

>Stop thinking, Sister Gabriel.
>*(to Y. MARY)*   And stop scratching!

GABRIEL:

>But what is she supposed to do now? She's a music teacher.

AGNES:

>And what are you, her mouthpiece? And a math teacher. She'll do two hours of math instead.

GABRIEL:

>No more music in the halls! It's a tragedy!

AGNES:

>Remember your vows!

GABRIEL:
>But the next time they come around, they'll make the opposite recommendation. We've seen it before Aggie. Why should we put up with this?

AGNES:
>You know why, Gabriel. At least you knew yesterday and the day before, and every day before that for the last ten years. Because it is our duty. Isn't it, Sister Mary? Isn't it?

Y. MARY: *(finally)*
>Yes, Mother Agnes.

AGNES:
>Then tell that to Sister Gabriel.

Y. MARY:
>It will be all right, Sister Gabriel. At least God has spared the pottery.

GABRIEL:
>God has nothing to do with it!

AGNES:
>One more thing before you storm off, Gabriel. Mr. Cameron has brought news from the reserves. It seems that Alice Paul's father is dying.

Y. MARY:
>Will she make it home in time to see him?

AGNES:
>She's not going. The Department does not think it's wise. It's a long way and they think it's risky. They're afraid that she'll revert to type and we'll lose her.

Y. MARY:
>But it's her father!

AGNES:
>He's too far gone. There's nothing anyone can do.

GABRIEL:

>What's happening to us? Dancing around to the whims of mean-spirited little men who don't even like children.

AGNES:

>Some of us like them far too much!

>*GABRIEL leaves.*

STEIN:

>You know when I'm not taunting nuns for burning down schools, I defend native people. Alcohol charges, fights, juvenile delinquents . . . I know some of my clients would have loved to see the place burn. Did anyone help you?

MARY:

>Leave me alone.

>*GABRIEL is moving around her pieces of pottery, humming a tune.*

STEIN:

>I'm no expert but I'd say that when people do things like burn down schools, they're making some kind of statement. Psychiatrists would go so far as to say they are asking for help. Were you asking for help, Sister Mary? Were you angry? Were you lashing out? Say something!

>*Y. MARY enters room where GABRIEL is looking out of the window.*

Y. MARY:

>Alice Paul has gone.

>*GABRIEL does not respond.*

Y. MARY:

>Did you hear me? Alice Paul has run away.

GABRIEL:

I know. I helped her. It was one of my little missions.

STEIN:

Were you angry? This is the age of protest. Did you burn down the school in protest against what went on in there?

GABRIEL:

Mary, you're glad she's gone, aren't you? Oh Mary, I did the right thing, didn't I? Admit it or it will eat you up.

AGNES enters while GABRIEL is speaking.

GABRIEL:

They can't lock up children. They can't lock up your voice so that you can't sing. I did the right thing, didn't I?

AGNES:

Answer her, Mary.

Y. MARY turns away.

AGNES:

Why, Gabriel?

GABRIEL:

Because I'm not sure anymore Aggie. Sometimes I wonder if we matter to God at all; if He has any idea that we are locked away in here. Suddenly I just had the need to unlock the door and let Alice go free.

AGNES:

Oh, did you? Well, because of your pitiful needs there will be no more picnics, or walks, or retreats, or trips to the city, no more little freedoms, just a long hard endless winter stuck away in this . . .

GABRIEL:

>Her father is dying! Let's not think of ourselves. She has been stalking back and forth in front of the window for a week like a caged animal.

AGNES:

>And we've all been praying for her. The rest is up to God. And now Mr.Cameron's dogs.

GABRIEL:

>I pray that we as Holy Sisters may draw together in solidarity

AGNES:

>I pray that we may draw closer to God.

>*Y. MARY very agitated.*

GABRIEL:

>I pray that we will not turn a blind eye to these childrens' plight. Help me Mary.

AGNES:

>I pray that you remember your sombre vows. Be still Mary.

GABRIEL:

>I pray that even though we have forfeited our own families, we'll have the compassion to allow others to . . .

AGNES: *(interrupts)*

>I pray that the rules of . . .

Y. MARY:

>You're not praying! You're fighting! Let the poor child go home!

>*GABRIEL squeezes Y. MARY's hand, victorious.*

GABRIEL:

>Thank you!

GABRIEL runs off, leaving AGNES and Y. MARY.
The sound of the dogs barking.

STEIN:

I'm sorry I bothered you. You stopped by the old
Indian school on a May evening and torched the
place and you don't want to talk about it. That's
understandable. Especially to me. All I know about
nuns, you could put on the head of a pin. For all I
know, you may have straightened this away with
your God already. I'm going to suggest that they
hand you back to Mother Agnes . . . get the Catholic
church throwing it's weight around . . . it's all smoke
and mirrors anyways . . . .

AGNES:

You can go back out there, Mary. It's not too late.
You haven't taken your final vows.

LOUIS:

I love you Mary. *Stay sitting*

AGNES:

There's probably a young man back home who you
could pick up with. Is that what you want?

Stand
LOUIS: *Well thought out*

I want to marry you, Mary and have a whack of kids,
go fishing in the spring, and duck hunting in the fall.
I 'll work at Henderson's garage, then take it over when
he croaks. You can do the books Mary, 'cause you're
so smart. Don't say no just yet . . . just think about it.

Y. MARY:

I need time to think.

AGNES:

Alice Paul is not being allowed to go home because there
is no home to speak of. Her parents are of a roaming
nature. The best we can do is to give her Christian values
so that she can see a better path for the future . . . .

45

Y. MARY:

She needs to hold her father's hand while he's dying. She needs someone to sing her nursery rhymes and stroke her hair and tickle her. She needs someone to love her. That's what she needs. Not all this gobbledegook . . . about better paths!

AGNES: *(a pause. Studies her)*

You miss your mother, don't you?

Y. MARY:

Don't change the subject.

AGNES:

Tell me about her.

Y. MARY:

Leave me alone.

AGNES:

She was kind, patient, and beautiful, wasn't she?

Y. MARY:

Yes.

AGNES:

She loved children didn't she?

Y. MARY:

With all her heart.

AGNES:

But they devoured her.

Y. MARY:

She gave everything she had.

AGNES:

Your mother was a good woman.

Y. MARY:

My mother was a saint.

AGNES:

> She wasn't a saint, Mary. You know all of the saints.

Y. MARY:

> I need silence.

AGNES:

> Your mother wasn't a saint. Your mother was one of God's ordinary foot soldiers.

Y. MARY:

> Silence.

AGNES:

> She was ordinary. She was weighted down with ordinary human frailties and weaknesses.

Y. MARY:

> And you aren't? Sneaking cigarettes when you think no one's watching; grabbing up all the potatoes, bullying Gabriel, marching around like one of my brother's tin soldiers, spying on everyone!

AGNES:

> And I do penance hourly for my transgressions. I work hard and I move steadily upward.

Y. MARY:

> She worked hard!

AGNES:

> But she couldn't completely surrender to the Lord, could she? She had sixteen children and a hungry husband.

Y. MARY:

> She did everything she could.

AGNES:

> But God is looking for the extraordinary, and that's why you came here. Not to be ordinary. You fled from that, didn't you? You knew where your

47

mother's goodheartedness got her. It killed her. And if you'd stayed with whoever it was . . . you might have ended up exactly the same. Except there's one difference. Your mother had faith burning inside her, didn't she, and you're still looking for it.

Y. MARY: *(takes time to answer)*
She told me I could be a star in the night sky but that I'd have to find my own light.

AGNES:
And you came here looking for that, didn't you?

Y. MARY:
Yes.

AGNES:
Tell me.

Y. MARY:
I used to see the Indian children working up here on the hill on my way home. I love children too, just like she did. I thought I could teach them to sing and love music, just like she taught us. I thought by helping them I'd find that light; that feeling. I would find God's unending love.

AGNES:
And you will someday Mary. If you are faithful, if you are patient, if you wait and listen, God will come to you. He will give you the grace to do great things in His service. But only if you let go of emotions and desires and human attachments.

Y. MARY: *(a pause)*
What about Sister Gabriel?

AGNES:
Sister Gabriel is being challenged spiritually and now she is going through a dark night. We will pray for her but we can't pander to her. She must find her solace in God.

The dog's barking ends. GABRIEL walks back in.

GABRIEL:

They've found our little Alice.

STEIN begins to leave

MARY:

No! Wait!

STEIN stops, turns.

GABRIEL:

They cornered her in a barn, shone a big flashlight in her eyes as if she were a criminal. I don't know what to do now, how to think, how to feel. Help me, Mary.

Lights up on LOUIS

AGNES:

Don't lose it, Mary.

MARY:

It's not straightened away with . . . . God.

STEIN:

I don't understand.

LOUIS:

I love you, Mary.

AGNES:

Don't let it get away from you or you're no good to anyone.

MARY:

I came back to see if Gabriel's tulips had come up. I went inside to pray . . .

STEIN:

Did God tell you to torch it?

49

MARY:

No! No one told me to torch it. It just happened.

STEIN:

You must have brought the gasoline.

MARY:

I didn't

STEIN:

But you must have planned it?

MARY:

I didn't.

LOUIS:

I love you, Mary.

MARY:

No!

AGNES:

Don't lose it, Mary.

MARY:

I didn't.

GABRIEL:

Hold my hand, little Mary.

Y. MARY:

No! Leave me alone!

Y. MARY/MARY:

Don't come to me. Go to God. It was wrong to help Alice!

MARY puts her face in her hands.

MARY:

I hear voices when I don't want to. I became
confused. Plunged into darkness. The fire provided a
wonderful light. But it's dark again.

GABRIEL's arms swinging in silhouette . . . the sound of all of her pottery shattering. Then silence.

STEIN:

I'm not sure this is a legal problem.

Act Two

Lights up on STEIN and MARY.

STEIN:

I'm not a shrink, Sister Mary. I think it would help if you saw one.

MARY:

No.

STEIN:

The department has a couple who they use all the time. I could give one of them a call. Sometimes they turn lights on in peoples' heads and they . . .

MARY:

No! I don't believe in psychiatrists, Mr. Stein. I go to God when I need "lights turned on."

STEIN:

But there seems to be a bit of a power failure.

MARY:

I guess so.

STEIN:

So what now?

MARY:

You could talk. Just talk.

STEIN:

Just talk.

MARY:

Just talk.

STEIN:

Winter's over. I hate Canadian winters. They're like traffic jams, piano lessons. My car doesn't start in cold, wet weather. I get stuck everywhere. I know all of the Automobile Association tow-truck drivers by first name.

I moved outside of town last fall to an old farmhouse because I wanted to slow down, become more laid back, on account of Marie, but now she's telling me that I should be more communal, less isolated. This winter I shared the place with mice, river rats, bats . . . since it's been getting warm, the bats have been slipping through the cracks between the walls and the attic and coming in for visits. When I come home late at night, I carry a tennis racket. So much for communal.

MARY:

Mothballs.

STEIN:

Pardon?

MARY:

They hate mothballs. Put them in the cracks and they'll go live somewhere else.

STEIN:

Really? I'll try that. Thank you.

MARY:

You're welcome.

STEIN:

Why don't you talk now.

MARY:

I have nothing to talk about.

STEIN:

Tell me what the school was like before you burned it down.

MARY:

Leave me alone.

STEIN:

It's your TURN, Sister Mary! Were there little water fountains?

MARY:

One on each floor.

STEIN:

Green walls?

MARY:

Yes.

STEIN:

And washrooms that smelled like . . . antiseptic?

MARY:

Borax and lye.

STEIN:

I heard it called the Resie.

MARY:

On rainy days, Sister Gabriel called it the soggy dungeon.

Lights up on GABRIEL wandering around swatting flies. She is wearing bedroom slippers.

STEIN:

Who cleaned those million windows?

MARY:

The older boys. Five times a year.

STEIN:

> I bet they loved that.

MARY:

> They didn't mind it. We all worked hard. We all had to pull our weight.

STEIN:

> Did you all eat together.

MARY:

> Girls together. Boys together.

STEIN:

> You really scalped them, didn't you?

Give her her moment

MARY:

> There were 150 children, Mr. Stein. Have you ever had headlice?

The sounds of the school begin to come back to MARY. The sweet, clear sound of the native girl singing a hymn, as in the beginning; then intrusive rock music begins to block it out. The music is heard only by MARY and it is bothering her.

STEIN:

> Did they all wear . . .

MARY:

> Balls and chains? That's what you want to ask, isn't it?

STEIN:

> Uniforms.

MARY:

> Of course they wore uniforms! Good sturdy ones that could be washed hundreds and hundreds of times. Why are you asking all these questions? Because you want to criticize.

AGNES:

> Hold on Mary.

56

MARY:

You're like a child poking at a dead bird in the yard.

STEIN:

I don't need this shit.
(starts collecting up stuff again)

MARY:

Don't swear in my presence.

STEIN:

I'm gone.

MARY:

Just don't criticize. That's all people seem to want to do these days. Condemn and criticize.

STEIN:

And what about you? Wasn't burning down the school a rather critical act?

The sound of rock music on a radio becomes too much for MARY. The sound of a pointer being banged against a desk.

MARY: *(shouts)*

Stop it! Turn that off! If you don't turn that radio off I'll smash it into a million pieces!

A loud bell rings. STEIN is unaware of the bell, Mary's shouting, the rock music, the other reality which MARY has entered.

STEIN:

Who is Alice, Sister Mary? You mentioned the name Alice.

MARY:

Alice Beaver, Alice Young, Alice Allen, Alice Goo Goo, Alice Christian? There were dozens of Alices and all of them . . . .

STEIN:

All of them what?

*Lights up on GABRIEL and AGNES who are in their
prayer stations. MARY also begins responding to AGNES'
call to prayer.*

AGNES: *(begins prayer under their conversation)*
Hail Mary, full of grace, the Lord is with thee, blessed
art though amongst women, and blessed is the fruit of
thy womb . . . [*Stand*]

*Lights up on Y. MARY. ~~LOUIS walks~~ back towards her;
stands watching her.*

MARY:

Holy Mother of God pray for us sinners now and in
the hour of our death . . .

STEIN:

All of them what?

MARY turns back to STEIN.

MARY:

Dear souls.

STEIN:

I don't know what that means.

LOUIS: ~~Scratching~~

You mean little buggers.

STEIN:

Why don't you say what you mean?

MARY:

Please, please give me strength, give me patience, give
me more love, dear God. Forgive me for I have raised
my voice at a child again and have had unkind
thoughts towards them because I do so hate their
music . . . and they show not the slightest inkling of . . . .

Standing?

LOUIS:

> Respect? I remember necking in the field in full view of Sister Justinian.

MARY:

> Give me Peace! Give me peace from . . . . Dear Lord please still the disturbing thoughts within me and help me keep my calm demeanour . . . .

LOUIS laughs

MARY:

> And please, please make me free of this little twitch in my left eye during math especially. Do I need to wear glasses, oh please God, I don't want to wear glasses . . . that would be the last straw. In Jesus' name . . .

GABRIEL:

> God, *(long pause)* Emma Stevens stood next to me at Mass and put her little hand in mine. I let her keep it there throughout the entire service. I didn't think you'd mind.

AGNES:

> In the year of our Lord nineteen hundred and sixty nine, I pray for wisdom to guide my beloved sisters around the political shoals and heathen souls of the Canadian government and Vatican Two. We are all being sorely tested, Lord. Give me the right words to explain what is happening.

GABRIEL:

> God, when it was time for the children to leave, Emma Stevens turned to me and whispered "Your face is like the Moon, Sister Gabriel. It looks like white cheese." Then she ran away laughing all the way down the hall.
>
> *GABRIEL puts her fingers up to her face.*

AGNES:

Give me the humility to entrust what lies ahead into
your hands, but knowing something of the world as I
do, I pray for the ability to adapt when necessary in a
Christian fashion. In the name of . . .

GABRIEL:

White cheese.

*GABRIEL does the sign of the cross. Picks up her fly
swatter and walks out. AGNES meets up with MARY and
GABRIEL*

AGNES:

How are you this fine day, Sister Mary?

MARY:

One hundred and ten percent thank you, Mother
Agnes.

AGNES:

You look a little tired around the eyes. Are you taking
on too much again?

MARY:

Only because there is so much to do.

AGNES:

God asks for only 24 hours a day from us, Sister
Mary.

GABRIEL:

Mother Agnes, do you think my face looks like white
cheese?

AGNES:

More like alabaster, Gabriel. *(takes the fly swatter
gently from her hand)* Sit down, please. Father Martin
has a little thought for us this morning about . . . throwing
open the doors. *(begins to read)*
    "We live in complex troubled times. Rebellious
youth, drugs, trips to outer space, go-go dancers,

Pierre Trudeau . . . . How can we better learn what is going on around us? How can we better learn to shed God's special light . . .''

AGNES hands out some magazines. MARY takes hers rather tentatively.

AGNES:

Father Martin has given us a year's trial subscription to *Time Magazine* and *Reader's Digest*. Here are the first two issues. And we will be able to listen to the radio in Community for one half-hour a week. Put them aside now please and let's talk about any problems which have arisen this week with the children. Sister Mary?

MARY:

The usual battles with the No Coat boys. I've gone to God for guidance.

AGNES:

Perhaps it's time to send them to Father Martin. Anything else?

MARY:

No, Mother Agnes.

AGNES looks at her for a while, MARY uneasy under her gaze.

AGNES:

And you, Sister Gabriel?

GABRIEL: *(still flipping through* Time *magazine.)*

Hazy McKay is becoming a woman. Poor little soul. She's behaving strangely, skin all covered with big red . . . . There's a picture of a woman here without any clothes on except for two little paper flowers on her . . .

AGNES:

> Put it away now, Gabriel. Perhaps Anna could make up a baking soda scrub.

GABRIEL: *(closes magazine)*

> Yes, that would be a good idea, probably. *(opens magazine)* Tits.

AGNES: *(closes magazine emphatically. To MARY)*

> I hear that Betty Simons spent time in the soap room yesterday.

GABRIEL: *(looking at cover now)*

> There are people hijacking planes and taking hostages.

AGNES grabs the magazine from GABRIEL.

AGNES:

> Let's not talk any further about it 'til Community. *(to Mary)* I'm wondering about the reason.

GABRIEL's attention distracted by a fly.

GABRIEL:

> May I get that one, please Mother?

AGNES hands her back the fly swatter.

MARY:

> I found her in there on two occasions with Peter Prosper with the light off. I was fed up with her insolence. So I yanked him out and left her inside.

AGNES:

> With the door locked and the lights out. For five hours.

GABRIEL:

> Hostages.

MARY:

> I was hoping to teach her a lesson.

AGNES:

A rather harsh one, Sister Mary, don't you think?

MARY:

Perhaps it was . . . in hindsight.

AGNES:

Pray for patience.

MARY:

I do, believe me I do.

AGNES:

Retreat is coming up. Winter's almost over. Soon we'll be outside again enjoying the fresh air. Yes?

MARY nods. GABRIEL floats about, swatting flies.

STEIN:

Why did you become a nun, Sister Mary?

GABRIEL:

Got it!

MARY doesn't answer.

STEIN:

Know why I became a lawyer? Because I wanted to be like Derek Hammer. He was the guy living in the apartment next to my mother's. He had a red sportscar and a beautiful red-haired girlfriend and was always on the news defending scoundrels in four-hundred-dollar suits. That was my idea of heaven.

MARY laughs.

STEIN:

And here I am, driving a ten-year-old Volkswagen beetle, in rural Nova Scotia, defending Indians and farmers and . . .

MARY:

Why are you so cynical about everything?

STEIN:

That way I'm never disappointed.

MARY:

Always glib, Mr Stein.

STEIN:

You're starting to sound like Marie.

MARY noticeably embarrassed.

STEIN:

But you're not.

MARY:

When I was in grade five, I had a teacher named Sister Justinian who had a face as smooth as an ocean pebble. She was the same age as my mother but she didn't have a line on her face and she never looked tired or unhappy. She was loved and admired by everyone.

STEIN:

She probably went home at night and kicked her dog around.

MARY:

Mind your tongue!

AGNES:

Pray for patience.

MARY:

You're not a Christian, Mr. Stein. I don't know what you believe in, what you follow.

STEIN:

Simon and Garfunkel. Leonard Cohen. Bob Dylan.

MARY:

I'm not familiar with those names.

STEIN:

You're kidding!

MARY:

No! I am not kidding!

STEIN:

They're modern day prophets.

MARY:

And is disdain and cynicism also modern day?

STEIN:

Nope! Philosophy 101. You're not exactly the picture of serenity yourself.

AGNES:

Is something bothering you, Mary?

STEIN:

Where did that darkness come from?

MARY with AGNES, a stack of books in her hand.

MARY:

I will be needing new songbooks. These are so torn, I've had to drop some hymns entirely because they're unreadable.

AGNES:

Well that's no good.

AGNES takes some books, starts looking through them.

AGNES:

"Ave Maria" has not fared well at the hands of your students.

MARY:

> I've been doing my best to cut and paste for a couple of years . . .

AGNES:

> I know you have, Sister Mary.

MARY:

> But some have no binding left to tape.

AGNES:

> So I guess the time has finally come . . . except there is no money in the budget for any more songbooks.

MARY:

> But if our task is teaching children, we need our tools, don't we? I can't keep control of my classes if I'm constantly taping letters back into the words of songs.

AGNES: *(sharply)*

> They should know the words by now! I'm sorry. I'm tired of all the cutting and pasting too. Perhaps next year will bring a change. Hope springs eternal. It's unfortunate that God doesn't live in Ottawa.

> *MARY doesn't move.*

AGNES:

> Is there anything else?

MARY:

> I read something in *Reader's Digest* which distressed me.

AGNES:

> Perhaps you should go to Father Martin for relief.

MARY: *(flares up)*
> No! I mean, it's not anything like that.

AGNES:

> Well, what is it then?

MARY:

It was the story about the Sister of Saint Rita.

AGNES:

Why did that distress you?

MARY:

How could someone stop being a nun after twenty-five years and take up flying airplanes?

AGNES:

A vocation is not for everyone. Often it takes a long time to understand that. Sometimes the values out there are tempting and people aren't that strong.

MARY:

It's unfathomable to me. To me, it would be like cutting off an arm or a leg . . . no, it would be even more than that. It would be more like being blinded. Don't you think?

AGNES:

Not everyone is blessed with as fervent a sense of mission as you, Sister Mary.

MARY:

I guess not.

AGNES:

Perhaps you should go back to the Psalms for a while.

MARY:

I'd like that.

AGNES:

And now I want you to go and fill your students' heads with music and mathematics and not your own with all this worldly claptrap!

MARY:

Tell me about the world, Mr. Stein.

STEIN:

The world. You've heard about the war . . . that I'm not in?

MARY:

Why aren't you?

STEIN:

'Cause I don't believe in killing people. And besides, it's not my war, it's someone else's war. If anyone owns a war. What else do you want to know?

MARY:

Are you a hippie?

STEIN; *(laughs)*
Yeh, I'm a hippie. I wear blue jeans on weekends, I don't trust anyone over thirty, I'm growing my hair long, I'm going to a rock concert this weekend with Marie and we're going to tune in, turn on, drop out . . . let the sunshine in . . . .

MARY is watching STEIN intently.

STEIN:

You don't know anything about that stuff, do you? Neither do I really. It's a crazy lonely place. You haven't missed much.

MARY:

You remind me of another young man I used to know.

STEIN:

What happened to him?

MARY:

He stayed young and I got old.

STEIN:

You're not that old.

68

Stand up

LOUIS comes up behind Y. MARY who is singing
"Somebody Loves Me." SR

LOUIS:

Why are you always singing?

Y. MARY:

D'you really wanna know?

LOUIS:

Yeh.

Y. MARY:

Promise you won't laugh.

LOUIS:

Cross my heart.

Y. MARY:

'Cause it takes me away.

LOUIS:

Thanks a lot.

Y. MARY:

I didn't mean that. I mean . . . it's like the prayers in
mass. It gets me closer to a feeling. Sometimes when
I'm singing, I start getting this picture of myself,
standing in a little moon-shaped beam of light in a
smokey club and I'm wearing a black dress and I've
got bare shoulders and a white gardenia in my hair
and my arms are floating through the air like
swans . . . and everyone is looking up at me . . .
loving me . . . adoring me . . .

LOUIS starts to laugh.

Y. MARY:

Go to hell!

69

LOUIS:

I can't help it. It's funny. And it's just like you. Always two feet in the clouds. You're a long way from beautiful, Mary Buchanan; you're pretty in a way that I like, but you're not beautiful. And you smell like baking soda not gardenias and you got a smudge of something on your shirt that moves around each time I see you. It IS funny! You know it is. Otherwise you'd be hopping a bus to Montreal instead of to the Motherhouse. Come to think of it, there's not much difference between the two . . .

Y. MARY starts to leave. LOUIS grabs her, holds her arms.

Pull her

LOUIS:

Playful

What I wanna know is why you can't just stay right here on earth with me? You wanna be loved and adored? I'll love you. I'll adore you.

LOUIS starts kissing her. Kiss shoulder

Y. MARY: *(faint resistance)*
Stop that.

MARY: *(bothered by this memory)*
Stop that.

STEIN:
What?

LOUIS:
Only two days left, airy Mary.

LOUIS and Y. MARY start kissing. MARY getting more agitated.

AGNES:
Hail Mary, full of Grace, the Lord is with thee, blessed art thou amongst women and blessed is the fruit of thy womb Jesus . . .

70

GABRIEL/MARY:

>Holy Mary Mother of God, pray for us sinners now and at the hour of our death . . .

GABRIEL:

>Sometimes at night, when you're lying awake, you'll feel an ache somewhere . . . just treat it as sleeplessness . . .

MARY:

>Dear God . . . do you remember Louis Lavers? He was a good person. He never went far in school, but he was smart in his own way . . . and he was a great kisser. I wonder where he is now. I hope you've looked after him.

AGNES:

>. . . when you enter the chamber of the Bridegroom, you may carry a shining lamp in your hand and meet Him with joy. May He find in you nothing disgraceful, nothing sordid, nothing dishonourable, but a snow white soul and a clear shining body.

GABRIEL:

>Just pretend there are big athletic woolly sheep jumping over these dreadful snake fences and count them as if your life . . . .

AGNES:

>Thy beauty now is all for the king's delight . . .

MARY:

>God . . . I heard a comedian on the radio last night from New York City. I was all by myself, I shouldn't have been listening, forgive me. *(pause)*
>He was pretending he was . . . You. The voice of God. Everytime he opened his mouth, the audience laughed. There was even a joke about a nun falling down the stairs. Forgive me Father, but I laughed at that. What is happening to me?

71

The sound of the native girl's voice begins again, singing a hymn. Clear, haunting. MARY is in spotlight, looking at the cross, very much alone now, absorbed in the voice.

MARY:

Do you remember Alice Paul? Of course you do. She must be a woman now. Where is everyone now? How are they all doing? Are you hearing me? Hello out there.

Lights change. The girl's voice begins to distort.

MARY: *(lashing out at a student)*

You are hopeless! You are a brute dull-eyed beast without the brains to understand even a simple addition of two numbers! And because you don't have the wit of a donkey, you may stand here and sketch a donkey for the next week on the blackboard. And turn your face to the wall!

Library. MARY stands at the window, her head resting against the pane, eyes closed. GABRIEL works at table.

GABRIEL: *(sings)*

"Somebody loves me, I wonder who, I wonder who it can be." I heard you last night. Sometimes I forget to take my pills. *(chuckles)* The walls have ears. No secrets. Not even at night. Especially at night.

MARY tries to escape.

GABRIEL:

Could you help me with this lesson.

MARY sits down, studies book in front of her. GABRIEL watches her intently with obvious affection.

GABRIEL:

You do look tired. You've got the yearnings, haven't you?

MARY:

Let's just concentrate on this, shall we?

GABRIEL:

Betty Simons is a good girl.

MARY:

Everyone is a good girl to you.

GABRIEL:

It's natural for a girl to feel an attraction for a young man. But sometimes it's hard to stand by and watch her when she starts to . . . .

MARY:

Because we worry about where her wantonness will lead her.

GABRIEL:

Of course. But sometimes one gets a little . . .

GABRIEL gets out a long stick and starts scratching her back.

GABRIEL:

Itchy.

MARY:

Try to concentrate!

They are quiet for awhile.

GABRIEL:

I'd like to be a guerilla. Not a gorilla, a guerrilla. I'd like to go underground. Imagine flying through the air like a bird. She said that she always had a dream of flying. A flying nun. I think its wonderful that she followed her dream. Don't you? To be free to swoop and soar below the heavens . . . .

MARY:

She left her vocation!

GABRIEL:
>But she followed her dream, just like we've followed
>ours. To love and care for children.

MARY:
>She's a traitor.

GABRIEL:
>What if God told her to go? If you don't spread your
>wings, how can you ever fly?

MARY:
>Don't talk nonsense!

GABRIEL:
>Maybe God approves of flying?
>He likes poetry, Ogden Nash . . . I'm sure he'd like
>Frank Sinatra . . . or whoever you were singing last
>night, if you'd only ask him.

MARY:
>I wouldn't ask him! I wouldn't ever bother him.
>Because God expects all or nothing, Gabriel. If we
>are truly doing God's work, we don't NEED Ogden
>Nash! Do you understand?

>*GABRIEL looks discouraged, confused. MARY, remorseful.*

>*A sound begins and becomes louder. It could be the hissing
>and clanging of a radiator. MARY and GABRIEL hear it.*

STEIN:
>Is there a friend you'd like to talk to? This Sister
>Gabriel that you've mentioned.

GABRIEL: *(distressed)*
>Mary?

STEIN:
>Is she a friend?

GABRIEL:

>It's started again.

MARY:

>Give me peace.

STEIN:

>Pardon?

MARY: *(back to Stein)*

>She is a Sister. We are all sisters.

STEIN:

>I see, but are you friends?

GABRIEL:

>The radiator has started hissing at me again. Just like
>a snake. And then the hissing takes the sound of a
>skipping rope . . . Fwap . . . fwap . . . fwap . . .
>fwap . . . which brings to mind the voice of my best
>friend Lucy Parker back on Garden Avenue . . . .
>"Gabbie . . . come out here please and play.
>Gabbie . . . I'm lonely. I miss you. "

>*STEIN notices that Mary is getting very distraught.*

STEIN:

>Are you all right?

MARY: *(working to block GABRIEL's memory)*

>Friendships are not encouraged, Mr.Stein. One is
>supposed to go to God for companionship.

STEIN:

>Hard to play pool with and share a pizza.

MARY:

>Always glib. Always mocking. When my students act
>that way, I know they're hiding something. I know
>they've done some nasty little act for which I will
>have to punish them.

STEIN:

It sounds like you enjoy that.

MARY:

I do not. But it has to be done. It's through discipline that they learn self-control.

STEIN:

And you are very controlled, aren't you? I can see all the little muscles working away in your face. Except when you bust loose and burn down the school.

MARY pounds the table.

STEIN:

What happened to your self-control?

GABRIEL:

I can't bear that sound. Someone's got to fix it.

AGNES has entered.

AGNES:

Got to fix what, Gabbie?

GABRIEL:

Those radiators.

AGNES:

I will.

MARY clenches her fists, closes her eyes.

MARY:

Sometimes we fall prey to one of the enemies of the soul — depression, despair . . .

STEIN:

So you recognize those feelings?

MARY begins moving about, agitated.

AGNES:
> Let's take our pill, Gabbie.

MARY:
> Of course we do but we have to turn our gaze back
> to God to overcome them. We have to bury our petty
> feelings and . . . memories and vanities and . . . .

> *STEIN puts his hands on her arms.*

STEIN: *(almost gently)*
> Why don't you start using the word "I"? I'm
> interested in YOU, Mary. Start with I, Mary
> Buchanan, 41, nun, teacher, arsonist, woman,
> want . . . I want . . . .

> *MARY looks frightened, closes her eyes.*

MARY:
> I want . . . you to hold me.

> *STEIN stunned, loosens his grip on her arms. MARY
> pulls away.*

MARY:
> I'm sorry.

STEIN:
> It's all right.

MARY:
> No it isn't.

STEIN:
> Yes it is. That made some kind of sense.

MARY: *(head down, murmuring)*
> What kind?

STEIN: *(uncomfortable)*
It was . . . spontaneous. *(Then not unkindly)*
Look, I don't think I can do any more for you. I'm going to call Anne Bishop, the other duty counsel in my office, and fill her in on your case.

MARY: *(after silence)*
That's the wall, isn't it, that Marie talks about?

STEIN:
I just don't think I can do any more for you. I've got my own problems.

AGNES:
Curiosity is to be avoided at all costs.

MARY: *(after pause)*
What are they?

STEIN:
Why do you want to know?

MARY:
I'm trying to understand . . . something, Mr. Stein. Anything. I'm not doing very well at it lately. And it's your turn, isn't it?

STEIN looks at her for a long time.

STEIN:
They want me to come home this weekend. Come home.

MARY:
Who does?

STEIN:
My father and his lovely wife. They want me to come on home and get to know my half-brother . . . the young Tyler. It's his birthday. Balloons, sticky faces. Goo, slobber, five years old and cute as a button. Come on home.

MARY: *(encouragingly)*
        That sounds like fun.

        STEIN just glares at her.

STEIN:
        "Just forget about the crummy childhood you had,
        kiddo, just come on home." Two weeks with my
        depressed night-shift nurse mother, then right into
        his little love nest where he and his cheery girlfriend
        were too busy fondling each other to notice that my
        socks didn't match, that my acne cream and
        homework were at "her" place, that I had no friends
        except the bus driver. And then they got married.

        STEIN seems absorbed in his thoughts.

MARY:
        I've read that that's very common now, second
        marriages.

STEIN: *(not listening)*
        Didn't even invite me to the wedding. They did it out
        of state at her parents' place — said they thought I
        wouldn't want to go, thought I would feel funny!

MARY:
        Maybe you would have.

STEIN:
        Bullshit! They were the ones who felt funny! I was
        dying for a big sweaty family to get into, dying to
        have my mug grinning in a million wedding pictures.
        Dying for it. And then they just went away. Said I
        needed the stability of one home. Bullshit! They
        didn't want to be bothered with me. "Goodbye
        fourteen-year-old fuckup. We're going off to find
        ourselves."
           But it's all water under the bridge now. Come on
        back into the fold. Get to know the young Tyler.
        Bring your girl friend, she'll appreciate him. Let's just

rewind. Wipe out the ugly bits, sing happy
birthday . . . makes you wanna puke. *(slams his hand
down on the desk)* Do you think I should go?

MARY:

I don't know. I truly don't.

STEIN:

Do you think you can just wipe out the ugly bits?

*AGNES brings out a letter from Father Martin, reads it to
MARY and GABRIEL.*

AGNES:

The Department has communicated to Father Martin
that there will be no further use of the strap in
managing the children. A lighter touch is in order
now in keeping with the tone of the time and a
brand new decade.

Silence.

AGNES:

It seems that Liberalism is the new word from on
high

GABRIEL:

Hallelujah.

AGNES:

Any other comments? Sister Mary?

MARY looks bothered

MARY:

"A teacher's knowledge is barren without the love —
patient and stern and sometimes steely — which
pushes each student to each one's highest
capablities." That was drummed into me when I first
arrived. We all know what STEELY means. It means
Discipline. What happened to that?

AGNES:

> Nothing's happened to it, Sister Mary. It's just that it's important for us to grow and change and not be hidden away . . .

GABRIEL:

> Barren:

MARY:

> The rules are there to help us avoid contamination from the world. What happened to that?

AGNES:

> Nothing's happened to it. But it is now felt that less discipline provides a better environment for children. It will give them more freedom to learn what we are trying to teach them.

MARY:

> Freedom to be lazy, rebellious, disrespectful. You haven't taught for a couple of years, Mother Agnes.

AGNES: *(sharply)*

> Because I've been too busy moving us into the twentieth century!

MARY:

> I'm sorry, Mother Agnes. Sometimes I admit to becoming discouraged, confused.

AGNES:

> We must all pray for patience.

STEIN:

> Who was Alice? I want you to tell me about Alice.

AGNES:

> Do you remember her, Mary? Alice Paul?

MARY:

> Of course.

AGNES:

> Maybe this will boost your spirits. Here's a letter from her, addressed to the Compassionate Sisters of St. Anne.

MARY: *(pleased)*

> May I open it?

AGNES passes MARY the letter, she opens it excitedly.

GABRIEL:

> May I put it in my cigar box?

MARY: *(reading)*

> "Dear Sisters, it is with great difficulty that I take up pen and try to write this letter to you. I still think of you all the way you were back then, when I was small and you towered over me, but you too have grown older and I wonder the point of this. But it must be said . . . ." *(MARY stops, reads on silently)*

AGNES:

> Has something happened to Alice?

MARY:

> Is this some kind of horrible joke? *(reading)* She says that she still has nightmares every night about the school, 15 years after, filled with the sound of the nun's heels coming along the hall towards her and the doors slamming shut over and over!
>
> What is this Mother Agnes? Where did this come from?

AGNES: *(upset)*

> Put it away, Mary.

MARY:

> "Whenever anyone asks me what it was like in there, I set the record straight about you all . . . empty vessels of meanness, Sisters of the Dark House . . . ." She wants

us to reply? To answer her charges? She says there will
be more letters, more charges? What is she talking about?

GABRIEL:

The Dark House.

MARY:

I don't understand, Mother Agnes.

AGNES:

Someone's put her up to this.

MARY:

Alice was devoted. Obedient.

AGNES:

Put it out of your mind, Mary.

MARY:

She loved it here. She even asked me once if I
thought she could become a Sister. And I told her if
she loved God and was obedient, someday it might
be possible. I didn't think there was any harm in
giving her hope.

GABRIEL:

Goodness no.

MARY:

I know it was wrong but I took her cakes.
I sang to her and stroked her hair after her father
died. She loved me for that. I was like her mother.

GABRIEL:

But you weren't.

MARY:

I never told anyone this but one day in chapel I
looked over at her, singing, her little face turned up
towards the cross, her eyes shining with light from
the candles, her sweet clear voice rising up into the
darkness, and suddenly I felt a warmth about my

shoulders like a heavy cloak. I knew that God was in the room with me . . . finally.

GABRIEL:

Oh, little Mary!

MARY:

Then right after that, we got her the job cleaning for Doctor Henderson . . . We were all tickled pink that things turned out for her, remember? But I never forgot that clear sweet voice. I kept it right here. I worked harder than ever, I buried my frustrations, my loneliness . . . I forged ahead.

It's all lies. Alice loved me. God loves me. What's happening, Mother Agnes? Help me.

AGNES:

Of course she loved you, Mary. But when she went back out there, the pressure from her upbringing was more than she could bear. We did our best. But we can't work miracles. Alice just didn't have the fortitude to withstand it.

GABRIEL:

Who does? I'd like to be a hippie. Free love. No strings attached.

AGNES:

We must pray for her still. We must hope that the Lord will give relief to her wounded soul. Are you all right?

MARY closes the letter.

STEIN:

Talk to me, Mary. Who was Alice?

MARY:

A poor unfortunate who lost her way. Who didn't have the moral fortitude to stay the course.

Stand and face Y. Mary

LOUIS:

Gobbledegook!

STEIN:

What's underneath all of that?

GABRIEL:

They hold hands, they kiss all the time whenever the spirit moves them. They don't just go through the motions. Wouldn't that be heavenly?

MARY:

Stop!

Y. MARY walks up to LOUIS.

Y. MARY:

The bus is late.

LOUIS:

Always is.

Y. MARY:

I'm so nervous. I didn't sleep at all last night.

LOUIS:

Neither did I.

Y. MARY:

I'd better get out to the road and wait. Goodbye Louis. I'm going to miss you.

She goes up to him, gives him a kiss, starts off.

LOUIS:

Mary, if you don't come to your senses soon, I'll have to take out Margaret McKinnnon. She's always after me.

Y. MARY:

That's okay, Louis.

LOUIS: *exaggerate my movements and*
Mary? I believe in God but not what people have
done to him. *expressions*

Y. MARY:
I gotta go.

LOUIS:

Kiss?

urgently

no kiss? realistic?

Mary? I was thinking about something last night that
really scared me. What if after you're in there awhile,
you find out God doesn't wanna have anything to do
with places like that - but it's too late - you're stuck
in there hating it and I'm hooked up with Margaret
McKinnon for the rest of my life selling her dad's
goddamned tractors . . .   (grabs her for one more
kiss) I've got this ache, Mary . . . and there are no
days left. You sang them all away.   *Sit down*
Sound of a belt coming down against a table. Silhouette of
MARY whipping someone.

MARY:
Ingrates! You are all little ingrates! Full of lies and
lust . . . flaunting yourselves, sneaking about . . .
draining the very life from us . . . . You never knew
what it was to truly believe. The beauty of belief! The
beauty of sacrifice.

GABRIEL: (starts reciting poetry to block out the sound of
the whipping)
"Thou still unravished bride of quietness, thou foster
child of Silence and slow time . . . "
Don't you ever hurt, Aggie? Even just a little?

AGNES:
The purpose of discipline is self-control. If you lose
control, you are no good to anybody. If we lose
control, we . . . .

AGNES' shoulders slump, she sits down behind her desk.
MARY is shaking, her fury spent.

STEIN:

What happened to Alice?

MARY:

She was a wayward girl who reverted to type.

STEIN:

That is the ugliest phrase I have ever heard. No wonder they say the things they do.

MARY:

And what DO they say? You've been dying to tell me. Spit it out!

STEIN:

They ate rat poison and cut notches in their arms so they could go out to the hospital. It was a prison.

MARY:

It was their home! It was their refuge.

STEIN:

From what? From their families, their mothers and fathers?

MARY:

Their homes were unfit. There was abuse.

STEIN:

They were whipped within an inch of their lives in there.

MARY:

We disciplined them. We tried to help them cope with the world.

STEIN:

Helped them fit into the lowest rungs of society. Took them away from all that was good and natural to them . . . their family, their language, their customs!

87

MARY:

> We touched them with our love.

STEIN:

> You never say the other word, do you?

MARY:

> What other word?

STEIN:

> Hate.

MARY:

> The school was their salvation.

STEIN:

> Did they program that word out when you entered?

MARY:

> It's only in the reconstruction of events that things
> fall apart for them. They forget the bright things, in
> the face of the bleakness. They forget picking wild
> flowers in the fields and berries in the tall grass and
> playing hide-and-seek with Gabriel and music and
> pottery. Someday they will remember how much
> they cherished us, loved us, respected us. It's only in
> the reconstruction that things fall apart . . . .

STEIN:

> And did they fall apart for you? Is that why you
> burned down the school?

MARY:

> I am waiting to see God's plan.

STEIN:

> You're floating out to sea.

MARY:

> We don't see everything at once. We get glimpses,
> little bits of light, little bits of hope, then it's dark
> again. But there is a master plan; the design of God's

providence. Only God sees it all and understands it all but it will all become clear to us in the fullness of time.

STEIN:

God hasn't got a plan and he's got no mercy! He doesn't give a damn about poor little Indians or devoted simple-minded nuns or pimply-faced kids from New York either. He's a joker and he's got a shitty sense of humour!

MARY:

You are a non-believer. A lost cynic. You know nothing about this!

STEIN:

I know what I never felt. I know that I wanted my father's love so bad that when I heard they were having a baby, I put all my faith into wishing the little creature ill for nine whole months . . . and lo and behold, it came out in the fullness of time, except that it wasn't all there, it was all screwed up mentally . . . and now I've got to live with that for the rest of my goddamned . . . . Hey . . . don't pity me! It doesn't matter. Mental retardation is sort of IN right now. They still love the poor little sonovabitch more than they ever did me.

It's your turn now, Sister Mary. What are you hiding?

GABRIEL is turning a piece of pottery over in her hand. MARY comes in, doesn't immediately see AGNES.

MARY:

Betty Simons has run away. We've got to tell Mother Agnes.

AGNES:

I already know.

MARY:

> It's my fault. I lost my temper. I whipped her. I
> know that it was wrong to use the whip on her. I
> lost control, I must do penance . . . I must be
> punished. We must get the dogs.

GABRIEL:

> Let her go. We all want to run away, Mary,
> sometimes. We all want to be free. I pray that we can
> finally let these children go free.

MARY:

> Help me, Mother Agnes.

GABRIEL:

> Vessels of meanness.

MARY:

> We've got a mission here and we've got to carry it
> out.

GABRIEL:

> Sisters of the Dark House.

MARY:

> Help me, Mother Agnes.

GABRIEL:

> Alice was right. We knew in our hearts but we
> buried it too deep and it lay in wait to sabotage us.

MARY:

> Shut up.

GABRIEL:

> God knew it too. That's why he left . . .

MARY:

> Shut up!

GABRIEL:

> He probably left with Alice Paul when she went off
> to clean Doctor Henderson's . . .

MARY: *(cutting GABRIEL off)*

> Traitor! That's what you are! A traitor to God.

GABRIEL: *(devastated)*

> No!

MARY:

> A crazy old bat full of tranquillizers and
> gibberish . . . no use to anyone let alone God!

GABRIEL:

> No!

MARY:

> Why didn't you leave back then when you found out
> you had so little faith?

GABRIEL:

> Because of you, little Mary. Because I loved you.

> *MARY stares at GABRIEL in horror, disbelief. GABRIEL*
> *pulls something out of the sleeve of her habit.*

GABRIEL:

> Do you like my little fish?

> *MARY turns to AGNES for help.*

MARY:

> We must call Mr. Cameron to bring in his dogs. Betty
> climbed out of one of the side windows. She'll be
> heading over the field. Why are you just standing
> there? Why aren't you doing something?

AGNES:

> Father Martin has advised me not to go after
> runaways.

MARY: *(disbelief)*
         Why not?

AGNES:
         The school is closing, Mary. They'll be going to the
         provincial schools like everyone else. Indian children
         will be integrated into the white society. It will give
         them more opportunities. It will be good for them.

MARY: *(whispers)*
         And what about us?

LOUIS: Loudly TURN IN towards audience
         Without ever having . . . .

AGNES:
         There are other missions. There is a school in Truro
         needing your services. Gabriel will come with me to
         the Motherhouse. I'll take good care of her. It's a
         brand new world for us, Mary. There are new
         challenges out in the community to do God's work.
         You're smart, you'll do well. Say something, Sister Mary.

MARY:
         You're very good at this business, aren't you?

STEIN collects his things.

STEIN:
         Spilling my guts to a nun on a Friday night. Cheaper than
         a shrink. See you around, Sister Mary.

STEIN starts to leave. MARY calls to him.

MARY:
         Mr. Stein? God forgives us for going astray. You can take
         comfort in that.

STEIN:
         Right. Bye-bye, Sister Mary.

MARY:

> Mr. Stein? Your father took it away and now he wants to give it back.

STEIN stops, turns. They look at each other.

MARY:

> Why don't you help him. What is there to lose? Why don't you forgive him.

STEIN puts down his briefcase.

STEIN:

> Why did you do it?

Sound of fire and ALICE's voice singing comes up again under, as in the beginning.

GABRIEL:

> I'll miss the floors. We had the shiniest floors in North America.

AGNES:

> Don't think about it.

MARY shakes her head.

GABRIEL:

> What will happen to all the little frame beds?

AGNES:

> Scrap.

STEIN: *(cutting through the inner voices)*
> Mary! Why did you do it?

GABRIEL:

> He's been silent for so long, it's like he's mad at me.

STEIN: *(urgent)*
> Sister Mary?

MARY:

I got confused. I heard voices.

STEIN:

What were they saying?

GABRIEL:

We're like a wave moving where God blows us, aren't we, Mother Agnes . . . the school and then . . . .

MARY shakes her head.

GABRIEL:

We're like icebergs.

STEIN: *(slowly)*

Why did you burn down the school?

MARY:

Because it caused such pain. It hurt so much.

MARY beginning to break down.

STEIN:

Go on.

MARY:

Because I hated it.

STEIN:

Go on.

GABRIEL floats over to the window.

GABRIEL:

Do you think the tulips will come up without us watching them?

MARY: *(finally)*

Because I broke Gabriel's heart.

(Long long pause)

MARY:

I came back to see if her flowers had come up. They were everywhere. Like red and yellow ribbons winding through the crabgrass. Food for the soul. The front door was open. There were some Indian children at the end of the hall. When they heard me come in they ran away and left behind a container of gasoline and a box of matches. I sprinkled the gasoline on the window blinds the same way I'd seen Tommy No Coat do in grade five, then lit the match. Only this time, Sister Agnes didn't come with a bucket of water to put it out. And then it was gone.

MARY turns to STEIN.

STEIN:

Thank you Sister Mary.

He reaches out his hand.
After a moment, MARY takes it.

The lights go down.

THE END